Reflections

FINDING THE COURAGE AND FAITH TO
TRANSFORM THROUGH FORGIVENESS

Gina Geronimo

Madison + Park

This book is dedicated to my family, whose unwavering support has been the bedrock of my journey through motherhood. Each day, you have inspired me to grow, to learn, and to embrace the beautiful chaos that life brings.

To my sons, Kairo and Gino—my heart swells with gratitude for the joy and purpose you've brought into my life. You both have transformed my existence in ways I never thought possible. The honor of being your mother has not only deepened my love but has also provided me with a profound opportunity for healing. Through the unconditional bond we share, I have been able to confront and break the generational cycles that once felt insurmountable.

Kairo, your laughter lights up my world, reminding me to cherish the present and find joy in the little things. Gino, your curiosity and resilience inspire me to be my best self, encouraging me to explore new horizons and embrace change. Together, you have taught me the true meaning of freedom—freedom to love deeply, to forgive wholeheartedly, and to live authentically.

As I navigate the complexities of motherhood, I am continually reminded that this journey is not just about nurturing you both but also about nurturing myself. Your presence has ignited a fire within me, pushing me to reclaim my identity and pursue my dreams with purpose.

To my family, thank you for believing in me, for your endless patience, and for being my greatest cheerleader. Your love fuels my passion and gives me the courage to share my story with the world. This book is a reflection of our journey together, a testament to the lessons learned, and the love that binds us.

With all my love,

GG

Declaration

This book entails the reality of womanhood; especially motherhood. As the navigation of the journey can sometimes be difficult—the purpose of defining oneself is the destination we seek as we evolve. To reach the destiny of self-love & worth, forgiveness & accountability, opportunities & choices, etc. is the daily goals towards healing and success. The ability to completely surrender at whichever stage you currently find yourself by accepting what is; in order to thrive forward is the ultimate goal in living an intentional life.

This book will entail journal reflections so as you read along you can tap within to seek the answers that are already within you; along with gems of advice and personal stories in between chapters. The purpose of this book is to encourage you to push forward in profound and new ways in which you may discover about yourself.

Contents

Chapter 1

Trauma, Triggers, Tests

When reflecting on our traumas, triggers, and overall stressors caused by events, circumstances, or life te it is essential to "accept" the presenting factors in order to cope and achieve positive outcomes. Humanity has encountered such challenges, each at different levels, depending on the season in which one endures the event or circumstance that arises. There are no coincidences in the tasks assigned to one's purpose as we evolve collectively. People enter our lives for a reason, a season, or a lifetime. As we traverse different cycles along our journey, we must learn to value our experiences and the lessons and blessings that unfold during our healing efforts.

Building relationships has been the foundational aspect of our existence since conception. The importance of these connections may serve spiritu, physical, mental, social, and emotional purposes, which can either break us or elevate us into the next seasons of our lives. The categories listed below manifest throughout our lifetimes in various forms, creating lessons or opportunities for growth and blessings.

Some spiritual traumas and cycles continue through generational bloodlines, perpetuated unconsciously through learned behaviors. As these repeated cycles occur, we must identify them and shift the energy spiritually so that the inner work can begin, enabling us to break the chains that bind us to limitations. Internal awareness is crucial before behavioral shifts and outward results can be realized. The spiritual journey is one to be embraced as we heal and trust in the process of breaking cycles, ensuring that future generations will face fewer battles and be fulfilled in their divine purpose.

Here are three examples:

1 **Religious or Spiritual Abuse:** This can occur when a person experiences mistreatment, manipulation, or coercion within a religious or spiritual context. Such abuse can lead to feelings of guilt, shame, and a distorted sense of self-worth. It may also result in loss of trust in religious or spiritual institutions and authority figures.

2 **Loss of Faith:** When an individual experiences a significant crisis of faith or loses their belief in a higher power or spiritual framework, it can lead to deep existential questioning, feelings of isolation, and a sense of purposelessness. This loss can impact their relationships, moral compass, and overall sense of meaning in life.

3 **Cultural or Ancestral Disconnection:** Being separated from one's cultural or ancestral spiritual practices can lead to a perception of disconnection, identity crisis, and a feeling of not belonging which can result in a lack of grounding, confusion about one's values, and a search for belonging and identity.

The physical attraction amongst humans allows chemistry to encourage one another to unite. The physical appearance of people has allowed us to identify common interests and relate to the outer world. Physical attraction is the most common pre-judgement process in which humans can be deceived by being physically attractive in a great way to gain attention, but other elements play a role in sustaining such attraction. Physical attraction and appearance can influence connections by sparking initial interest in potential romantic partners, impacting how others perceive and interact with you in social settings, and even affecting networking opportunities in professional environments where first impressions are crucial.

The famous quote: "not everything that shines is gold" holds value in the physical realities of where our pain can cause confusion at times. For example: How can my family members do this to me? Why would my ex-husband make this decision? My child would never do that? Although, most of the pain we experience is caused by people we love or those close to us. We physically can't comprehend the why but must separate ourselves from what is being experienced and tap into our emotional realm to feel and process. Examples of physical attraction/appearance could include facial attractiveness, body proportions, grooming, personal style, as well as traits like confidence and posture. However, it's important to note that physical attraction is subjective and can vary from person to person. Physical attraction and appearance can also play a role in various aspects of life, such as forming initial impressions, influencing personal relationships, and even impacting professional opportunities like job interviews or networking events.

The emotional level (matters of the heart) is a powerful one. Humans display different emotions as moments occur throughout the days, months, and years. The emotional stages vary according to the wins and losses that arise along the journey. Studying the patterns of one's emotional state will allow us to identify the triggers where we then can heal through the shift of emotions by choosing. It is imperative to know oneself deeply to master the emotional intelligence that through time will save us as tests arise. For example: engaging in negative encounters can trigger someone to become extremely emotional, possibly causing harm or even death. When you can control your emotions during chaos it gives you time to think before acting based on those temporary emotions.

The social (interactions/communication) component allows us to verbalize our emotions in a mature way. The goal is to communicate to be not only heard but to be understood—a big difference. Many people listen to respond and do not understand; causing a lack of comprehension due to the overall miscommunication society displays today. For example: if you buy a coffee, taste it, and dislike how the coffee you brought tastes. The moment you communicate there is a dislike; a defensive energy arises where the worker takes it personally and misses the point of customer concern and satisfaction. If we simply learn to truly listen, we as a society would be able to help one another and make the world a better place.

Below are three examples of how the social component allows us to verbalize our emotions in a mature form to be understood:

1 **Active Listening:** Engaging in active listening during conversations allows individuals to truly understand and empathize with the emotions being expressed. Paraphrasing and reflecting on what the other person is saying demonstrates a genuine effort to understand rather than just formulating a response.

2 **Using "I" Statements:** When expressing emotions, using "I" statements such as "I feel" instead of placing blame or making assumptions about others' intentions can help to communicate emotions in a more mature and non-confrontational manner. This approach encourages a deeper understanding of personal feelings.

3 **Seeking Clarification:** Asking clarifying questions and seeking to understand the perspective of the other person demonstrates a commitment to clear communication and understanding. This can help to bridge the gap of miscommunication and ensure that emotions are delivered and comprehended accurately.

These examples emphasize the importance of not just speaking, but actively seeking to understand and be understood in social interactions.

The mental (matters of the mind) attraction is the only way to maintain connections through memories, encounters, and experiences. The mind is a port where the majority of our life's perspective is fueled. It is vital to educate ourselves when addressing toxic thoughts, dealing with insecurities, and learning to be satisfied with ourselves. Many live in the illusion of people, places, and things that will temporarily quench the thirst of that state of mind. Many people seek temporary satisfaction or fulfillment through material possessions, relationships, or experiences. Examples include buying expensive items to feel successful, seeking validation through social media likes, or engaging in fast relationships for companionship without a genuine emotional connection. The goal is to be driven by those illusions and work hard to make them a reality.

Another example is someone who may be happy when they are with their partner. The illusion of associating happiness only to that person; when the reality is that everyone is responsible for their happiness—another person, place, or thing should not be the entire reason for an individual's happiness. These should be considered as contributing factors to the internal root of the way we perceive ourselves mentally. Addressing toxic thoughts, and insecurities, and learning to be satisfied with oneself often involves a combination of self-reflection, education, and seeking support. Here are several ways to educate oneself in this process:

1 **Self-awareness:** Start by understanding your thoughts and behaviors. Educate yourself about the nature of toxic thoughts and insecurities. This might involve reading books, listening to podcasts, or attending workshops that focus on self-awareness and mental well-being.

2 **Therapy or Counseling:** Seeking professional help from therapists or counselors can provide valuable education on how to recognize and

address toxic thoughts and insecurities. Therapy can also provide tools to improve self-esteem and self-acceptance.

3 **Mindfulness and Meditation:** Learning about mindfulness and practicing meditation can help in recognizing negative thought patterns and developing a healthier relationship with oneself. There are plenty of resources, including apps and online courses, that can guide you through these practices.

4 **Positive Affirmations and Gratitude:** Educate yourself on the power of positive affirmations and practicing gratitude. Understanding how these practices can shift your mindset and promote self-acceptance is crucial in the journey toward satisfaction with oneself.

5 **Reading and Research:** Engage in reading materials that focus on self-love, self-compassion, and personal growth. There are plenty of books and online resources that can provide insights and practical strategies to address insecurities and toxic thought patterns.

6 **Community Support:** Joining support groups or communities where individuals share similar experiences can provide education and emotional support. Learning from others who have successfully navigated similar challenges can be incredibly valuable.

Keeping in mind that addressing these challenges is a process that takes time and effort. It's important to be patient and kind to yourself throughout this journey.

These spiritual, emotional, physical, social, and mental connections are built based on interaction (sometimes are not meant to be understood right away). People play roles in our lives which impacts our abilities to think, feel, and behave according to the lessons and blessings that unfold throughout the relationship. Various roles and examples can significantly impact the way a person thinks, feels, and behaves when trying to connect lessons and blessings in relationships.

1   **Mentorship:** A mentor can provide guidance and wisdom, offering valuable lessons and insights from their own experiences. By observing and learning from a mentor, individuals can develop a deeper understanding of relationships and personal growth.

2   **Parental Influence:** The way parents or guardians model behavior and communicate can greatly influence a person's approach to relationships. Positive parental influence can instill values, empathy, and communication skills that impact how individuals navigate their relationships.

3   **Personal Experience:** Lessons learned from personal experiences, both positive and negative, can shape an individual's approach to relationships. For example, a difficult breakup

might teach someone about resilience, while a supportive friendship might highlight the importance of empathy and understanding.

4 **Spiritual or Religious Guidance:** Spiritual or religious leaders can offer teachings and principles that guide individuals in understanding the significance of lessons and blessings in relationships. These teachings often shape beliefs about forgiveness, compassion, and love.

5 **Therapeutic Relationships:** The relationship between a therapist and a client can serve as an example of healthy communication, empathy, and trust. Through this dynamic, individuals can learn how to navigate their relationships more effectively.

These roles and examples can serve as powerful influences, shaping an individual's mindset, emotional responses, and behaviors within the context of their relationships. Recognizing and understanding these influences can be instrumental in connecting the lessons and blessings within relationships.

Relationship is the ability—to relate, the moment we no longer relate or outgrow people our cycles of life begin to change. Acknowledging the sacrifices, struggles, and pain and the acceptance process of how things that happen to us are blessings in disguise. These "negative" experiences mold our character on the journey to be able to handle tests differently and blessings with grace.

Growing up, I endured the trauma of becoming a parentified child at an early age. Not having the full comprehension of the responsibilities that were projected onto me created an internal pressure that as a child I was not prepared to accept and embrace. I was forced to grow up fast to ensure the house duties, childcare for my brothers and other contributions were accomplished along with the expectations of achieving success. It all started when I was about 8 years old . . . after my mother birthed a new sibling into my life in which she needed my assistance with her new beginning in her motherhood journey. Although many of the responsibilities as a child has helped shape who I am today—by taking on such tasks that instilled a strong work ethic, responsibility, and the ability to manage multiple priorities effectively; as a child I did not have the maturity to understand these concepts in which made me feel unworthy, overwhelmed, frustrated, stressed, etc.

For example: As a 9-10-year-old little girl I would often ask myself "Why am I washing almost 10 bags of clothes for the entire household in the laundry mat" and then cry as I'm folding all the clothes while thinking about what other kids my age were doing. That was the awakening of how I knew that I was built differently. The rest was history—long story short I never really had a childhood. Being a parentified child can cause a range of emotional, social, and psychological challenges. These may include feelings of overwhelming responsibility, difficulty forming and maintaining peer relationships, struggles with personal boundaries, and potential impacts on mental health. Coping with parentified trauma can involve several strategies, such as seeking therapy to address and process the experiences, setting and maintaining healthy boundaries, practicing self-care, building a support network, and engaging in activities that promote self-expression and stress relief.

Journal Reflection: *A Letter for Mother*

Disclaimer: This journal entry below was the past version of myself which samples the anger and resentment I felt against my mother growing up. Today this is not the relationship we endure. Thank goodness for grace, forgiveness, understanding, and compassion as we intentionally continue to pour into our relationship. This is called healing!

Dear Mom,

As a little girl, I dreamed of becoming a general surgeon. I spent hours watching health programs, but as I grew older and faced challenges in my family, that dream started to feel distant. I took on adult responsibilities early, caring for my younger brothers, cleaning the house, and doing laundry. The emotional struggles around me affected my outlook on life. Despite these challenges, I tried to maintain a positive mindset, always hoping for better days. I've come to realize that these experiences have shaped who I am today. I'm actively working on healing and nurturing my spirit. For many years, I have carried feelings about our relationship. I often felt like my efforts went unrecognized.

There were times when I wished for a different reality, and my faith sometimes wavered. I remember moments that made me feel unloved or unsupported. My room became a refuge where I could express myself freely. I often felt uncomfortable when others entered my space, as it felt like an invasion of my privacy. Music provided a way for me to process my emotions, and those experiences taught me that material things don't hold lasting value. I struggled with feeling a lack of unconditional love, which has influenced my relationships. I often felt that my thoughts and feelings weren't understood, leading me to keep things to myself. The way I was raised has impacted my behavior, pushing me into survival mode.

While I faced difficulties, including moments of physical discipline, I understand that everyone has their own struggles. I recognize that you were raised in a strict environment, but I hope that future generations can learn from the past. I am committed to breaking the cycle of pain and ensuring that my future children experience a nurturing and supportive environment. All these years, I've pretended to forgive you, but today I've finally expressed everything I've held inside for so long. Now that I have voiced my feelings, I can genuinely forgive you, regardless of whether you accept it. What matters most is that I am finally true to myself. In the end, that's all that counts! Be free, live your life, and do what makes you happy! If you want to dance, then dance—stop worrying about what others think of you! It's not who we are but what we do that defines us. Love yourself and cherish every moment! As RahGor said, "Your location is not your destination." After this chapter of my life, tremendous growth opportunities await me now that I've taken this significant step toward true forgiveness. If it weren't for God, you, and my father, I wouldn't exist. Among countless others, I was chosen for a purpose. My mission in life is to fulfill that purpose.

If I've never said thank you, I apologize. Thank you for the struggles I faced at a young age; they prepared me for the real world. They helped me overcome challenges and take risks that have led me to this very moment. I appreciate your efforts in trying to shape my path toward success. With all due respect, I will now continue to carve my own journey—one that will be remembered and will impact lives around the world with my motivational and inspiring spirit. I will succeed—no excuses! I am not a victim of my life; my experiences have forged a warrior within me, and it is my greatest honor to be her, the person I am today."

Endure the journey as things are happening for us, not to us! I have the blessing of reflecting and measuring my growth through my journal entries. To have the ability to go back in time and see the transformation process through writing as the healing journey is never narrow. I encourage you to find a method that works for you identify deeply what is holding you back from your purpose and release the weight when you are ready. Choose today to let it go, accept and surrender. All traumas, triggers, and tests are puzzle pieces that make the beautiful picture you are meant to be.

Gina G Reflections

If you had the option of being born again or erasing parts of your life—which, would you choose? Why? Would it matter? The answer is NOT REALLY because if you were born again—you would have to live with a new set of traumas (maybe worse) and if you erase past traumas—you wouldn't have learned or gained the wisdom you have today.

Chapter 2

Surrendering to Your Power and Thoughts

The mindset is the engine that allows us to elevate based on emotions, discipline, and decisions. The powerful tool of thought influences the behaviors and actions that will impact the different outcomes along our journey. We can close the gap between the life we desire and currently living by the way we produce our thoughts and the thoughts we choose to believe. At times, we find ourselves beating up our positive thoughts from the mistakes we've made, and by not learning from past mistakes, we are robbing ourselves of the opportunity to make better decisions for our future. If we change our mindset, our actions will align to bring about positive results based on the perspective we choose to adopt in our lives.

Many times why people won't reach their true potential is because they are too attached to their past. We can't let attachment to the past hold us back from rewriting our stories as we embrace growth, challenges, and discomfort throughout the transition of our future. Although we are not in control of the past, the results, the future, what others think of us, and other people's opinions, we DO have the great privilege to control our thoughts, words, and responses and become self-aware of how we treat ourselves and others.

Personally, my family's expectations (college, degrees) discouraged me from pursuing my passion for hairstyling. It likely created barriers that hindered me from fully expressing my creativity and reaching my full potential in that field. As a talented stylist, who grew up in a family that limited my creative endeavors due to other priorities. The lack of encouragement and support in my formative years resulted with me struggling with self-doubt and never fully pursued my passion for hair/beauty. The fear of this experience of not being validated or supported held me back from fully developing my skills and reaching my full potential as a hairstylist in the future.

Growing up doing hair was therapeutic for me and recognizing the positive impact it had on my well-being was very important. As years passed; pursuing what brings me joy and serves as a form of therapy can be a powerful motivator to break free from past limitations and fully embrace my passion for hairstyling, speaking, writing, impacting others, and anything I want to accomplish within me. Overcoming these expectations and pursuing my passion could lead to a more fulfilling and successful lifestyle. As we embrace the difficult tasks, they stretch our abilities and refine our character. Don't just focus on the material rewards, but instead seek how you can serve others and make a positive impact. The truth and hope within us have a transformational effect on those around us. It is essential to strive for excellence while never shying away from challenges; for in those moments of difficulty, we truly grow and thrive.

To control your thoughts, words, and responses, you can consider mindfulness practices, cognitive-behavioral therapy techniques, and communication skills training. Here are some resources that may help in this area:

1 **Books:**

- *The Power of Now* by Eckhart Tolle
- *The Four Agreements* by Don Miguel Ruiz
- *Mindset: The New Psychology of Success* by Carol S. Dweck

2 **Courses/Workshops:**

- Mindfulness-Based Stress Reduction (MBSR) courses
- Communication skills workshops offered by organizations like Toastmasters International

3 **Videos/Online Resources:**

- TED Talks on mindfulness, emotional intelligence, and communication skills—Online courses on platforms focusing on mindfulness or communication techniques

4 **Apps:**

- Headspace or Calm for guided meditation and mindfulness practices
- 7 Cups for online therapy and emotional support

These resources can provide tools and strategies to help you develop more control over your thoughts, words, and responses, leading to improved communication and emotional well-being.

Journal Reflections: *A Heart Renewed*

January 4, 2023

As I continue my journey of healing and personal evolution, I find myself increasingly focused on renewing my love for God, for myself, and for others. With the dawn of the new year, I envision my heart transforming into something completely new—pure and white, as if born clean and untouched. This symbolic renewal is not just a fleeting wish; it is a profound intention that I am determined to manifest in my life. I long to fully embrace and receive the human embodiment of God's unconditional love. To do this, I recognize the need to release the barriers that have clouded my capacity to accept this love— doubt, worry, confusion, anxiety, and disbelief in the goodness that surrounds me. I am committed to peeling away these layers of negativity, allowing my heart to shine brightly and freely.

In this process of renewal, I am actively letting go of past burdens: worries that have weighed me down, traumas that have lingered too long, and negative emotions that no longer serve me. I am casting aside the need for control and survival energy that has held me in a state of constant tension. Instead, I am opening my heart wide to welcome new and magnificent experiences that await me. I am learning to forgive myself for the decisions I made when I was operating from a lower frequency. I acknowledge that those choices do not define me;

rather, they are part of my growth. I am worthy and deserving of incredible, everlasting love—love that is forgiving and nurturing. I am ready to invite into my life good-hearted people, uplifting places, enriching opportunities, and things that align with my highest good.

Continuing this transformative journey, I can physically feel the release of pain and tension within me. Every few hours, I sense a deep pressure pulling at my heart, a reminder of the hurt that is being released. I embrace this process wholeheartedly, with pure intentions and a deep desire for healing. Thank you, God, in advance for the love, peace, and joy that are unfolding in my life. I trust that by renewing my heart and opening myself to your grace, I will be able to experience the profound connections and blessings that await me. This is just the beginning, and I am ready for all that is to come.

Take Some "L's"

LIVE: Living freely and unapologetically in the present moment, irrespective of others' emotions, reactions, or perspectives, can be a powerful way to cultivate personal growth and happiness. It's important to prioritize your well-being and authenticity in your journey through life.

LOVE: Embracing love for the divine, the universe, oneself, and all beings, including those in need and nature, can foster a deep sense of interconnectedness and compassion that enriches our lives and the world around us. Love is a powerful force that can bring healing and harmony to all aspects of existence. Utilizing daily affirmations, scriptures, music, and other positive influences, as well as leaning on your support network, intuition, and personal well-being practices, can provide a strong foundation for navigating life's challenges and embracing personal growth. Trusting in yourself and the resources around you can lead to a more balanced and fulfilling life.

LEARN: Learning from both your own experiences and the experiences of others can provide valuable insights, growth, and wisdom that help you navigate life more effectively and make informed decisions. Embracing a mindset of continuous learning can lead to personal development and a deeper understanding of the world around you.

LAUGH: Finding humor in life's absurdities, enjoying the present moment, and not taking things too seriously can bring lightness and joy to your experience. Laughter can be a powerful tool for stress relief and positively connecting with others.

Being powerful within your thoughts is the ability to identify which thoughts, behaviors, choices, and pain belong to YOU. Understanding and respecting the thoughts of others without letting them overshadow our vision, goals, and dreams is crucial for maintaining clarity and focus in our lives. It's essential to strike a balance between understanding external viewpoints and staying committed to your path and aspirations. Those projections have nothing to do with us and everything to do with distractions along our journey.

The reflection of courage, mental endurance, and the presence of God held pivotal value in the moments of life difficulties back then. The ability to sustain mental strength co-existing with the infinite source of God will only create people of substance, which we lack today. What characteristics of people with substance carried back then that people today lack? I ask myself this because I embrace the presence of God—who is the source who has implanted the morals and characteristics in all realms of my life; mentally, physically, emotionally, and most importantly spiritually.

Recognizing that God is the infinite source of all things in your life and for the readers can provide a foundation of strength, guidance, and purpose. By deepening your connection with the divine, you can draw upon a wellspring of faith, love, and support that can inspire and uplift you in various aspects of your journey. This belief in a higher power can offer comfort, wisdom, and a sense of interconnectedness with the universe and all beings, guiding you toward a fulfilling and meaningful life.

To be a person of substance through the power of thought, one must possess qualities beyond knowledge and understanding. It requires strength, courage, leadership, and purpose to stand up for what is right, even when challenges in the community arise. This transformational drive cannot be accomplished by simply conforming to mirages of success, but rather by standing firm in one's convictions. Having faith in oneself and the power of God is essential for building mental resilience and thriving in life. While some find guidance through sermons, others can connect with their higher selves and God through personal experiences such as meditation, nature walks, acts of kindness, inspirational literature, mindfulness practices, or even through art and creativity. These diverse avenues allow individuals to deepen their spiritual connection and belief in something greater than themselves, fostering inner strength and a sense of purpose beyond traditional religious teachings.

The power of the mind strengthens the ability to resolve with the qualities of someone who is admired, respected, and influential. The ability to carry oneself with dignity, and respect to others and drive change through their actions. They not only embody the representation of God but also the phrase "actions speaking louder than words." Facts are pieces of information that can be objectively proven true or false through observation or experimentation. They are verifiable and often universally accepted, such as the fact that all humans have a heart. These factual truths serve as a foundation for knowledge and understanding in various fields of study and can help shape our perceptions of the world around us.

Knowing the truth, on the other hand, refers to a deeper understanding of reality or a situation. It goes beyond mere facts and involves personal beliefs, experiences, and wisdom. The truth may not be objectively verifiable, but it holds personal significance and can guide one's actions and decisions within thought processing. The statement "Knowledge is facts—truth is God" implies that knowledge is limited to what can be observed and measured, while truth transcends human understanding and is associated with a higher power or ultimate reality.

Surrendering is the act of letting go of control and allowing yourself to trust in a higher power or a greater purpose. The opportunity to surrender often presents itself in moments of uncertainty, challenges, or when we feel overwhelmed by circumstances beyond our control. By surrendering to our fruitful thoughts—those that stem from a place of purity and guide us toward our true selves—we can align with our authentic path and purpose. Surrendering to these thoughts allows us to embrace clarity, intuition, and inner wisdom, leading us toward growth and fulfillment. Moreover, surrendering to the flow becomes essential when we have given our all and have reached a point where further resistance seems futile.

This surrender to the flow involves letting go of resistance and trusting in the natural course of events, allowing life to unfold organically. By releasing our grip on outcomes and surrendering to the flow, we open ourselves up to new possibilities, growth, and transformation. As we embark on this journey of surrender, we are encouraged to release our need for control and embrace the unknown with faith and openness. Surrendering can be a powerful practice that invites us to trust in the process of life, let go of fear and doubt, and welcome the opportunities for growth and self-discovery that lie ahead.

My Personal Experience: *Surrendering to the River*

July 22, 2023

Rafting experience for Wale's birthday weekend . . .

This weekend, we (13 friends) endured our 4–5-hour rafting (divided into 2 groups) experience. We are close to the end; the excitement increases as if we are winning the race and celebrating our achievements. In seconds, that excitement shifted when suddenly the raft crashed into a huge rock wall—flew out the raft—where the pressure of speed took us underwater instantly. I am deep under. I never felt the ground platform for support to push myself back up. Here is where the power of my thoughts is tested as my life depends on it. I'm making my way up to the surface only to find myself under the raft. I'm trying to punch in various locations to find raft edges in hopes of open surface space.

Suddenly, I felt a push on my shoulders as if someone was weighing me down into the water almost drowning I shifted my circumstances and focused all my attention on my state of mind as I attempted again to come up to the surface (Literally telling myself to continue to hold my breath as long as I could and that I'm doing great remaining calm) the raft continues to block the surface—I failed again.

At this point, I tell myself to find peace in surrendering as I had no control of the situation I was in. As I tried for the third time, only to find myself stuck under the raft! At that moment I said to myself—my kids are safe at home! And completely surrendered—thanking God in advance for my life journey—in case I never made it out alive. My mindset provided me with the sense of knowing that panic or negative thoughts would have killed me faster. The power of my thoughts and applied faith (a mental attitude that clears you from fears) allowed me to remain calm under pressure while surrendering and releasing control of the outcome.

My mind, body, and spirit felt aligned. I finally see light as I open one eye slowly—as the voice of God assists me to look up and around. I rise to the surface only to see my sister, Welma, looking down at me on the raft with a very worried facial expression of desperation while pointing in the direction behind me as I'm trying to catch my breath for air. I turn around to find another raft with a group trying to assist—I grab onto the paddle and flow through the travel in the opposite direction to end on land. As the raft filled with water continued to push through the water making it very difficult to paddle for exit—my group and I were separated.

The girl was in tears as I sat there to reflect on the experience. She expressed her fear as she observed the impact from a distance encouraging her group to paddle with speed to assist our group. I was listening to her and soaking in my thoughts with heavy breaths to ensure I was alive. It felt like a vivid dream. I awakened to the interpretation of the test I felt I passed. How so? I was put through a spiritual test to not only check my mental power but also my applied faith under the environment in which I least thrive in "water" as I allegedly don't know how to "swim." In the past, this same scenario would've given me a panic attack underwater possibly causing instant drowning.

After reuniting with my group—there was a moment of understanding that although we had been working together for hours that urgent moment forced everyone to fend for their individual life. In speaking to Welma her perspective through her lenses gave her extreme concern of seeing everyone else rising to the surface one at a time and not seeing me until moments after . . . She explained feeling the anxiety of knowing that I couldn't swim, encouraging her to jump into the water in hopes of finding me. Through conversation, we established that everyone had to save themselves before thinking of others, so she returned to the raft and that's when she saw me and was able to direct me to assistance from the other raft.

Initially, it was difficult to assess the individuals in our raft by their strengths and weaknesses as it was a new experience for most which made it difficult in the beginning as we kept getting stuck on rocks, forced into different sides, etc. Those challenges allowed us to take a break mid-point (snack, hydrate, and regroup) to proceed in a strategic way to complete the task in a strong, productive way through COMMUNICATION. The reflection of staying present and surrendering to the unknown can bring about a sense of peace and serenity. By staying present, we can fully engage with the present moment and appreciate the beauty and opportunities it holds. Surrendering to the unknown involves letting go of our need for control and accepting that there are aspects of life that are beyond our understanding or influence. This surrender allows us to embrace uncertainty with openness and curiosity, rather than fear or resistance. Together, staying present and surrendering to the unknown can lead to personal growth, deeper connections, and a greater sense of trust in the unfolding of life's journey.

Having a growth mindset is crucial as it fosters resilience, a willingness to learn from failures, and a belief that abilities can be developed. It helps individuals embrace challenges, persist in the face of setbacks, and see effort as a path to mastery, ultimately leading to personal and professional growth. All of the past decisions you've made have contributed to your learning experiences allowing you to measure your growth and move forward in the path God has already created for us. Time is essential, especially God's timing. Realizing why having something when you're truly ready for it is so much better than receiving it prematurely and being overwhelmed. Timing is important, being ready for something is just as important as getting it. The importance of a positive and productive mindset allows us to receive experiences for our highest good with the sense of KNOWING in times when things don't seem aligned.

Gina G Reflections

What steps will you create to attain the ability to shift your mindset when people, places, or things do not meet your expectations?

Chapter 3

Mastery of Discipline

Discipline is key to success as it offers the structure, focus, and consistency needed to progress towards your goals. It enables you to prioritize tasks, stay motivated, and overcome obstacles, regardless of your aspirations' scale. Whether starting with small goals or pursuing big dreams, discipline guides you forward. Let's define discipline simply to ensure clarity and encourage personal growth.

To simplify, discipline is the compass that helps you step out of your comfort zone, explore new methods, and gain fresh perspectives on life. For instance, consider the misconception that attending college guarantees financial stability and success. In reality, success requires more than just a college degree. Let's back this up with concrete statistics and data. In each aspect of life—mental, physical, spiritual, emotional—balance is crucial for thriving. Let's call these aspects "realms" for diversity. For mental discipline, it means setting aside time for learning new skills. Physically, it could be maintaining a regular exercise routine, spiritually finding time for meditation, and emotionally, practicing self-care.

A misleading belief in society is that success is solely tied to a college education, which isn't always accurate. Take the example of garbage workers who, despite societal perceptions, often earn more than teachers. We need a diverse range of skills and professions for a functional society. Let's delve into the falsehoods perpetuated by certain philosophies, using concrete data on salaries, lifestyles, and more to debunk these myths. By understanding the truth, embracing self-improvement, and stepping outside their comfort zones, individuals can appreciate diverse experiences and interests to become more well-rounded.

Discipline transcends degrees and races; it's a daily decision to create and implement a strategy for personal growth and success. While discipline may look different for each individual, the formula for success is simple: do what works for you consistently until you achieve your goals. It's about making incremental progress daily toward your vision of a better self. We must acknowledge and support those who haven't followed traditional educational paths due to circumstances, fostering motivation and drive through diverse life experiences.

In today's world, the internet offers endless opportunities for personal growth and creativity, yet many conform to societal norms rather than exploring their full potential. The pressure and uncertainties of college can lead to emotional and financial stress, with job prospects dwindling and bills mounting, creating challenges for students.

As a first-generation college student, I believe college isn't a requirement for success but can be beneficial for personal growth and learning from diverse perspectives. Success stems from qualities like self-motivation, persistence, consistency, dedication, and openness to new experiences, essential for personal growth and achieving goals.

My personal discipline formula involves completing small tasks daily to achieve larger goals, much like the structure of a college education. The discipline strategies outlined below can benefit individuals from all walks of life, not just college students, to enhance focus, time management, and overall success.

1. **Establish a Schedule:** Create a routine that includes study time, activities, and personal time to develop good time management habits.

2. **Define Goals:** Break down your goals into manageable tasks to track progress and stay motivated.

3. **Avoid Procrastination:** Prioritize tasks and use techniques like the Pomodoro Technique to enhance productivity.

4. **Stay Organized:** Keep study materials organized using tools like calendars or apps.

5. **Seek Support:** Utilize available resources for guidance and additional learning opportunities.

Remember, everyone's path to discipline and success is unique. Find what works best for you and adapt as needed to navigate your journey effectively.

Journal Reflections: *Discipline Create Greater Opportunities*

April 4, 2022

Today, I find myself reflecting on the concept of discipline and how it intertwines with the hardships and struggles of daily life. It's a complicated relationship—one that is often tested by the diverse challenges I face. As I strive to achieve my specific goals, I am constantly reminded of the obstacles that stand in my way. Life is undeniably hard, and I often wonder how to navigate the complexities that come with it. Family struggles weigh heavily on my heart. Balancing my responsibilities as a mother with my personal aspirations can feel overwhelming at times. The demands of parenting require my unwavering attention, and while I cherish every moment, I also grapple with the longing to carve out time for my own growth. It's a delicate dance—one where I must remind myself that nurturing my own dreams ultimately benefits my family as well.

Workload is another significant factor. Juggling a job that often feels all-consuming leaves little room for me to pursue my passions. The hours spent at work can feel like they drain my energy and creativity, leaving me exhausted by the time I return home. I find myself questioning how to cultivate the discipline needed to push through these challenges and still make progress toward my goals. Time—my most elusive resource. I often catch myself wishing for more hours in the day. Between family obligations, work commitments, and the endless to-do lists, finding even a few quiet moments for reflection or learning feels like a luxury. I sometimes feel guilty for wanting to take time for myself, as if self-care is a selfish indulgence rather than a necessary component of my journey.

Limited resources also hinder my progress. I know that to assist others and become truly resourceful, I need access to opportunities and connections that can elevate me to the next level. While I understand that a degree isn't the only path to success, the reality of networking and building relationships can be daunting. It requires time, effort, and a certain level of confidence that I am still working to cultivate.

Despite these hardships, I refuse to let them define me or my journey. I know that discipline is not merely about maintaining rigid routines; it's about being adaptable and resilient in the face of adversity. Each challenge I encounter is an opportunity to grow stronger and more resourceful. I am learning to embrace the messiness of life while holding onto my dreams with determination. As I navigate this journey, I remind myself that it's okay to take small steps. Every day, I can choose to carve out a little bit of time for myself—whether it's reading, brainstorming ideas, or connecting with others online. I can use my experiences to inspire those around me, sharing my journey authentically and lifting others as I climb.

I am committed to mastering discipline, not just in the traditional sense, but in a way that honors my unique path. I believe that as I push through these struggles, the opportunities I seek will begin to unfold. I am ready to embrace the journey, knowing that each hardship is a stepping stone toward achieving the goals that matter most to me. And in this process, I trust that I will not only elevate myself but also create a positive impact on the lives of others.

Having a structured routine can greatly impact the speed and confidence with which you achieve your goals. A routine serves as a roadmap, helping you prioritize tasks and manage your time efficiently. By reducing decision fatigue and streamlining your workflow, you can accomplish tasks more quickly, leading to faster results.

A structured routine cultivates discipline and consistency, essential for sustained success. By engaging in productive habits regularly, you build momentum and a sense of mastery over time. This progress boosts your confidence and self-assurance, propelling you towards your goals. Additionally, a structured routine provides a sense of control and reduces anxiety by offering a plan to tackle challenges. With a clear roadmap, you approach tasks with a positive mindset, feeling prepared and empowered to overcome obstacles. Overall, a disciplined routine not only accelerates outcomes but also nurtures confidence, empowering you on your journey.

Gina G Reflections

What dreams, goals, or aspirations do you have that don't necessarily require a degree but instead demand discipline and structure to achieve? Where can you allocate discipline in your life to focus on reaching these specific goals?

Chapter 4

The Courage to Own Consequences

Taking full accountability for our decisions is crucial because it reflects our integrity and maturity. When we hold ourselves responsible for the choices we make, it shows that we understand the impact of our actions and are willing to face the consequences. Accountability allows us to learn from our mistakes, grow as individuals, and build trust with others. By accepting outcomes, whether they are positive or negative, we demonstrate resilience and adaptability. It enables us to move forward, make necessary adjustments, and strive for better outcomes in the future. Ultimately, taking full accountability empowers us to take control of our lives and create a path of personal and professional growth.

Taking ownership of your choices and being accountable for your decisions can greatly influence your future outcomes and lead to personal growth. It's empowering to realize the impact of the choices we make. Indeed, the power to shape our future lies in the choices we make today. By taking accountability for our actions and making thoughtful decisions, we can pave the way for a better and more fulfilling future. It's important to consider the potential consequences and long-term impact of our choices, as they can shape the path we take and the opportunities that arise.

With the global crisis that we face today, an example of a bad choice with long-term consequences is substance abuse which continues to have a significant impact on individuals and society today. It can lead to negative consequences such as health problems, mental health issues, strained relationships, financial difficulties, legal troubles, and decreased productivity. Additionally, substance abuse contributes to societal problems like crime, accidents, and healthcare costs. The opioid epidemic, alcohol abuse, and the misuse of prescription medications are some of the key challenges faced by society about substance abuse.

Another personal example that affects me directly could be procrastinating on important responsibilities at times which can result in missed opportunities, increased stress, and a pattern of poor time management that affects future goals and success. For me juggling increased responsibilities in motherhood while managing a limited schedule can lead to feelings of anxiety. The pressure to fulfill daily tasks, take care of my children, and work towards long-term goals within a restricted time frame can be overwhelming. My ability to sleep has been significantly impacted by the stressors of motherhood that has restricted me from achieving restful sleep. Mothers need to practice self-care, establish priorities, seek support from family and friends, and potentially consider time management strategies to help alleviate some of the stress and anxiety associated with managing multiple responsibilities. I address these stressors through relaxation techniques, establishing a bedtime routine, creating a calming sleep environment, and seeking support when needed to improve your sleep quality and overall well-being. It is important to embrace your ability to make impactful decisions and strive for a future that aligns with your goals and values.

Journal Reflection: *Learning with Lessons*

August 22, 2012

On August 17, 2012, I returned to New Jersey after a long summer of traveling between the Dominican Republic and Florida. My family was overjoyed to see me, and I missed them dearly. During my month-long stay in Florida, I became acutely aware of the number 817. Whenever I encountered it, I prayed for clarity, seeking to understand its meaning or message. I shared this with my sister and began keeping track of the people, places, and events associated with it. That summer was spiritually significant for me as I deepened my faith and learned to embrace the journey of life without expectations. I had gone to visit my sister in Florida, and it felt like a divine decision to buy a one-way ticket. This trip taught me the importance of staying present and fully engaged in the moment.

However, upon my return, I lost that sense of calm. Disobedience led me to make choices that nearly cost me my life. One evening, my cousin and friends gathered in the backyard, sharing stories, laughter, and good cheer. As the night went on, we spontaneously decided to go to a nightclub. We hurried to shower, dress, and get ready in just 20 minutes.

As we were about to leave, my mother asked me to stay home and urged me to heed her request. I remember looking at her and asserting my independence, reminding her that I was grown and capable of making my own decisions. We hopped into a BMW coupe, five of us in total. Shortly after we arrived at the club, my cousin realized she had left her phone at home and felt uneasy. She wanted to take a cab back, but I encouraged her to wait a little longer so we could all leave together. Eventually, she insisted on leaving, and I accompanied her outside to order a cab.

Ironically, our driver's friend decided to take us instead. As we exited the parking lot, the driver accelerated in reverse at about 80 mph, crashing into another car. In a matter of seconds, we found ourselves in a major accident, the car careening like a pinball between metal poles before coming to a halt in an isolated area.

In that moment, I spiritually recall entering a dark tunnel where moments from my life, from birth to the present, flashed before me. I vividly saw my mother giving birth to me. Suddenly, the physical vibration of my cell phone disrupted this vision, jolting me back to the terrifying reality: we were trapped, airbags deployed, the engine smoking, with no way to escape. A voice from the car alerted us that emergency assistance was on the way. At that moment, I felt the presence of God with us.

Firefighters arrived and used the jaws of life to free us from the wreckage. The EMS ambulance took us to the hospital, where we learned the extent of our injuries: broken jaws, shoulders, fingers, arms, swollen faces, and shifted necks. Despite it all, we were grateful to be alive.

As I lay in the hospital bed, I saw my mother, who looked concerned. She told me that she had been asleep when she dreamt I was screaming, "MOMMMMMMMYYYYY." This dream startled her awake, prompting her to call me repeatedly, sensing that I needed help. Her intuition and discernment likely saved my life, interrupting what could have been a tragic end. If not for her dream, I might have continued into that tunnel and experienced what I can only assume would have been the afterlife.

This experience taught me a profound lesson: while obedience is often viewed as an important virtue, disobedience can also yield valuable lessons. The date, August 17, serves as a powerful reminder of my near brush with death and the importance of listening to those who care for us.

Obedience can be defined as the act of following instructions or commands from an authority figure or a set of rules. It involves compliance, submission, and adherence to established guidelines or norms. Disobedience, on the other hand, refers to the refusal or failure to comply with instructions or rules, often as a form of rebellion or defiance against authority. In a spiritual sense, obedience can refer to following the teachings, principles, or commandments of a higher power or spiritual belief system. It involves aligning one's actions with the prescribed moral and ethical guidelines of that belief system.

1   **Challenging Authority and Promoting Change:** Disobedience can be a catalyst for questioning authority and challenging societal norms. Throughout history, acts of civil disobedience have played a significant role in driving social progress and advocating for justice. By disobeying unjust rules, individuals and communities can bring attention to important issues and inspire positive change.

2   **Cultivating Critical Thinking:** Disobedience can encourage critical thinking and independent thought. It prompts individuals to question the status quo, evaluate rules and regulations, and consider alternative perspectives. This can lead to personal growth, intellectual development, and the ability to make informed decisions.

3   **Individuality:** Disobedience can be an expression of one's autonomy and individuality. It allows individuals to assert their own beliefs, principles, and values, even in the face of societal expectations or pressure to conform. This self-expression can foster a sense of identity, authenticity, and personal empowerment.

4 **Learning from Mistakes:** Disobedience, when done responsibly, can provide valuable lessons through the consequences that follow. By taking risks and challenging established norms, individuals may encounter failures or setbacks. However, these experiences can offer important opportunities for growth, self-reflection, and learning from mistakes.

5 **Encouraging Ethical Decision-Making:** Disobedience can arise when individuals believe that a higher ethical principle or moral imperative supersedes adherence to rules or authority. In such cases, disobedience can serve as a moral compass, promoting ethical decision-making and holding individuals accountable to their values.

It is important to note that disobedience should be approached thoughtfully and responsibly, considering the potential consequences and impact on others. However, when used constructively, disobedience can serve as a powerful tool for personal growth, social progress, and the pursuit of justice.

Obedience can serve a valuable purpose in various contexts:

1 **Social Order, Safety, and Stability:** Obedience to laws, rules, and societal norms helps maintain social order, stability, and harmony within communities. It ensures that individuals act in ways that are beneficial for the greater good and prevent chaos or conflict such as following traffic laws or workplace safety guidelines.

2 **Efficiency and Productivity:** Obedience to organizational rules and procedures in a work setting can enhance efficiency, and productivity and improve overall success within a business or institution.

3 **Education and Learning:** Obedience to teachers and educational systems can facilitate effective learning, skill development, and academic success for students, providing a structured environment for growth and knowledge acquisition.

4 **Parenting and Child Development:** Obedience in the context of parenting can establish boundaries, instill discipline, and promote healthy child development by teaching children important values, behaviors, and responsibilities.

5 **Legal and Ethical Compliance:** Obedience to laws, ethical principles, and moral standards helps uphold justice, fairness, and integrity within society, fostering a sense of accountability and respect for the rule of law.

6 **Personal Growth and Development:** Following instructions and guidance from authority figures such as teachers, mentors, or supervisors can lead to personal growth and development.

Obedience in learning environments, for example, can help individuals acquire new skills, knowledge, and perspectives that contribute to their overall development.

Owning your decisions and becoming self-aware throughout the process is a powerful way to take control of your life and navigate it with wisdom. Through accountability, you can own your decisions, and you take responsibility for the outcomes and consequences. This mindset empowers you to learn from both successes and failures, and it encourages personal growth.

When you recognize that you have the power to make choices and take action, you regain control over your life. It allows you to shape your path with empowerment and make decisions aligned with your values and aspirations. Becoming self-aware throughout the decision-making process involves introspection and understanding your thoughts, emotions, and motivations. This awareness helps you make choices that are in alignment with your authentic self and reduces the likelihood of making impulsive or regretful decisions.

As you own your decisions and become self-aware, you embark on a journey of personal growth. You gain insights into your strengths, weaknesses, and areas for improvement. This self-awareness enables you to make more informed decisions and continuously evolve as an individual. Taking ownership of your decisions builds confidence in your abilities and strengthens your resilience. Even in the face of challenges or setbacks, you develop the resilience to learn, adapt, and course-correct, knowing that you have the power to shape your future.

Gina G Reflections

By embracing the wisdom and power to own your decisions and becoming self-aware throughout the journey; what mindset, goals, habits, and structure are you going to create to lead a more intentional, fulfilling, and authentic life for yourself? Create it NOW!

Chapter 5

Patience is Faith

Life often unfolds in ways beyond our control, presenting us with challenges, surprises, and moments of uncertainty. In these turbulent times, the virtue of patience emerges as a guiding light, illuminating our path with the gentle glow of faith. Patience can be defined as the ability to endure difficult situations without becoming frustrated or anxious. It is the capacity to accept delay, hardship, or uncertainty with grace and composure, recognizing that time is often an essential ingredient for growth and understanding. In the face of life's unpredictable nature, patience serves as a steady anchor, allowing us to navigate the storms with a calm heart and a clear mind.

To embody patience amidst the chaos of life is not merely an act of waiting; rather, it is a profound reflection of inner strength and resilience. It requires us to embrace the present moment, to be still, and to trust in the unfolding of our journey. By practicing this stillness, we create space for clarity and insight, allowing ourselves to step back and observe the larger picture. In this way, patience and stillness are intricately connected. Patience invites us to pause, to breathe, and to reflect, while stillness grants us the opportunity to listen to the whispers of our intuition and the subtle guidance of the universe. Together, they form a harmonious balance that empowers us to face life's uncertainties with a sense of peace and confidence.

To be patient is to surrender our desire for immediate results and to trust that everything unfolds in its own time. It is a conscious choice to let go of our need for control and to allow the universe to orchestrate its grand symphony. Each note, whether soft or loud, contributes to the beauty of the whole composition, reminding us that even in moments of discord, there is potential for harmony and growth. In the tapestry of life, patience weaves together resilience and faith, illuminating our path through every challenge and surprise.

In the silence of patience, we discover a sanctuary of peace and clarity, where doubts and fears fade into the background. This stillness is not an absence of activity; rather, it is an essential aspect of patience itself. Within this tranquil space, we nurture the seed of faith, believing in the unseen and trusting in the timing of our lives. Here, we surrender to the wisdom of the journey ahead, recognizing that patience is a dynamic force that requires us to be present and engaged, even as we wait.

As we embark on this exploration of patience as the embodiment of faith, let us understand that the art of stillness is intrinsic to the practice of patience. It is in this stillness that we welcome the lessons that unfold during our waiting periods, allowing us to cultivate deeper insights and understanding. By embracing the quiet moments, we open our hearts to the transformative power of patience, which guides us along our path toward our ultimate destiny.

In this light, patience, and stillness are interconnected, each enhancing the other. Patience provides the framework within which stillness can flourish, allowing us to navigate life's uncertainties with grace. Together, they become a profound expression of trust in ourselves and the greater journey, empowering us to face challenges with resilience and hope. In this sacred interplay, we find the strength to embrace the unfolding of our lives, knowing that every moment of waiting is an opportunity for growth and renewal.

Being still in faith while trusting the process to your destiny means maintaining a steadfast belief in your higher power or guiding principles, even when faced with uncertainty or challenges. It involves having confidence that the path you're on is leading you toward your ultimate purpose or desired outcome, and surrendering control over the timing and specific details of how things unfold. This state of faith allows you to remain patient, resilient, and open to the possibilities that arise along the way, knowing that there is a greater plan at work. It involves a deep sense of trust in the journey, even when it may not align with your immediate expectations.

Having faith means believing in and trusting something greater than ourselves, even when we lack clear evidence or certainty. It is the strength to embrace hope, persevere through challenges, and find solace in the unknown. Faith empowers us to transcend doubt, navigate uncertainty, and seek meaning and purpose in our lives. It is a beautiful expression of trust, resilience, and the belief that there is something greater than ourselves.

To the mother in distress, remain calm. Growing up in a two-parent household, I always considered marriage a revered commitment, particularly when children are part of the equation. At the time of being married to the father of my sons, escalating differences eventually led to the choice of separation and ultimately divorce. Juggling the responsibilities of being a new mother to two sons, along with working full-time, became a daunting challenge on most days. Striving to give your all consistently and staying optimistic amidst the turmoil, there arises an inner longing to comprehend the unfolding events and the emotions you are going through.

To safeguard the image, he presents to the public, I choose not to delve into the specific instances of past hurt that I've since forgiven and moved past. The following excerpts are entries from my journal, written during moments of despair, serving as a tool for reflecting on my progress and path to healing. It's crucial to note that my current outlook on the world is far from what it once was, and I now view those experiences with gratitude for shaping the individual I am today and am still evolving into. I am fortunate to maintain a healthy co-parenting dynamic, allowing my sons to flourish and develop into the precious gifts they are destined to be.

Journal Entry: *Mother in Distress*

February 12, 2019

It's truly saddening how our communication has dwindled, leaving me feeling disconnected, distant, and distressed. Despite being your "wife", it often feels like we're at odds, as your choice of words like, "bruh" and "fuck", has spiraled out of control. In an attempt to maintain peace, I send you blessings, but now I realize my silence isn't enough. My mind races, my heart races, uncertain if the decisions I've made were truly incomplete, resonating deeply within me. I grapple with loneliness, unable to confide in you. Ready for a battle, I look ahead, haunted by a persistent intuition that something is amiss. Enduring hardships for the sake of our children, I stand resilient. If we reach a point of no return, I hope we can part ways amicably, prioritizing our mental, physical, and emotional well-being. Our relationship, once distant, drew closer, only to reveal a stranger within my home. What does love truly mean? If you embody its definition, then I'd rather bid farewell to our love. I seek peace by nurturing our children with unconditional love and guiding them on the path of compassion. Writing serves as my solace, allowing me to release pent-up emotions without regret, enveloped in silence and prayers for the liberation of my soul. I trust in God's plan, taking life one day at a time.

Dear God, please cleanse my life of anything that does not align with your divine plan. I trust in your protection and guidance, knowing that I am shielded by your grace. I rebuke all negativity, envy, hate, violence, addiction, infidelity, depression, gossip, and drama from my life. I pray for inner peace, love, happiness, positivity, patience, freedom, and the acceptance of all that I deserve. Safeguard my blessings, especially my precious children; may your Holy Spirit watch over them. I am grateful for all that you have done and continue to do in my life. Grant me the strength to face each challenge, the wisdom to learn from every trial, and the purity of heart to forgive as you forgive me. I am humbled

*and thankful for the life you have bestowed upon me.
Amen.*

Journal Entry: *Emotions on Paper*

October 14, 2019, at 10:43 pm EST

To the father of my sons,

*Your actions have deeply wounded me. My heart is
in pieces, and the betrayal is undeniable. With your
disloyalty and untrustworthiness, you've shattered
the foundation of our marriage. Did you consider
our family when you chose to deceive and disrespect
me? Your actions have irreparably damaged our
relationship. I deserve more than what you've shown.
I refuse to be treated like the women you entertain—I
am a queen. You've made a mockery of our bond,
revealing a lack of regard for our history together.
Your behavior is a disappointment. By disregarding
our marriage, you've only showcased your weaknesses.*

*You failed to value and appreciate me as your
partner. Despite this, I will continue to prioritize our
children above all else. Forgiveness is not an option for
the disrespect you've shown me. Our marriage is no
longer sustainable, and, regrettably, our children have
been impacted by this turmoil. I hope you seek solace
in faith and find the strength to seek forgiveness. I
respect you as the father of our sons, but any further*

communication should be solely about our children.
Peace and blessings.

Sincerely, GG

P.S. Please refrain from replying.

Patience and divine timing play significant roles in our lives. Patience allows us to remain calm and composed while waiting for things to unfold naturally. It helps us avoid impulsive decisions and allows us to trust in the process. Divine timing refers to the belief that a higher power or a greater plan is guiding our lives. It suggests that certain events or opportunities occur at the right moment for our growth and well-being. By practicing patience and trusting in divine timing, we can align ourselves with the flow of life, allowing for greater opportunities, personal growth, and a deeper sense of fulfillment.

Different Ways to Practice Patience While Waiting and Believing

1. **Mindfulness Meditation:** Engage in mindfulness practices to cultivate present-moment awareness and patience. By focusing on the now, you can learn to accept things as they are without feeling the need to rush or control outcomes.

2. **Deep Breathing Exercises:** Practice deep breathing techniques to calm your mind and body during moments of uncertainty. Deep breaths can

help you stay grounded and patient while waiting for things to unfold.

.3 **Positive Affirmations:** Repeat positive affirmations that reinforce your trust in the process and your faith in the journey ahead. These affirmations can help you stay patient and focused on the bigger picture.

4 **Gratitude Journaling:** Keep a gratitude journal to reflect on the blessings in your life and the progress you've made so far. Cultivating a sense of gratitude can help you maintain patience and perspective during challenging times.

5 **Visualizations:** Use visualization techniques to imagine yourself being patient and trusting in the process. Visualize your desired outcomes and see yourself calmly navigating through obstacles with faith and resilience.

6 **Self-Care Practices:** Prioritize self-care activities that help you relax and recharge. Taking care of your physical and emotional well-being can enhance your patience and ability to wait with grace.

7 **Seeking Support:** Reach out to friends, family, or a support group for encouragement and guidance during moments of stillness. Sharing your thoughts and feelings with others can provide you with additional perspectives and strengths.

8 **Setting Realistic Expectations:** Practice setting realistic expectations for yourself and others. Understanding that things may not always go according to plan can help you cultivate patience and acceptance in the face of uncertainty.

9 **Engaging in Hobbies:** Immerse yourself in activities that bring you joy and fulfillment. Engaging in hobbies can distract your mind from impatience and help you appreciate the present moment.

10 **Learning from Past Experiences:** Reflect on past experiences where patience has served you well. Remind yourself of the times when waiting patiently led to positive outcomes, reinforcing your faith in the process.

By incorporating these practices into your daily life, you can cultivate patience as a cornerstone of faith, enabling you to navigate the stillness of uncertainty with grace and resilience. In the symphony of life, as we embrace the mantra "What's for me, won't ever miss me," we adopt a mindset of profound knowing amid the unknown. This belief becomes our guiding light, illuminating the path ahead with unwavering faith and trust in the unfolding of our destiny.

As we navigate the twists and turns of our journey, we are reminded that patience is not merely the act of waiting but a testament to our resilience and inner strength. It is in the moments of stillness, where faith takes root and blossoms, that we discover the beauty of surrendering to the greater plan at play. With each breath we take and each step we make, we embody the essence of patience as the cornerstone of our faith. By holding steadfast to the belief that what is meant for us will find its way to us, we find solace amid uncertainty and courage in the face of adversity.

So let us carry forward this empowering mindset of knowing in the unknown, trusting in the divine timing of our lives, and embracing the journey with open hearts and unwavering faith. For in the tapestry of our existence, every thread of patience we weave becomes a testament to our resilience, our growth, and our unyielding belief that destiny will never fail to find its way to us.

Gina G Reflections

As you contemplate the idea of embracing stillness while trusting the process of the unknown, ask yourself: In what ways can you cultivate patience and faith in your life journey, especially during moments of uncertainty and waiting?

Chapter 6

The Transformative Power of Forgiveness

Embracing changes, healing from trauma, and elevating into your purpose are all important aspects of personal growth and fulfillment. Embracing changes allows you to adapt to new circumstances, explore different opportunities, and learn from life's experiences. Change is inevitable, and by embracing it, you can open yourself up to growth and new possibilities.

Healing from trauma is a crucial part of personal well-being. It involves acknowledging and processing past experiences, seeking support when needed, and taking steps toward healing and self-care. By addressing and working through trauma, you can free yourself from its emotional burden and create a foundation for a healthier and more fulfilling life.

Elevating into your purpose means discovering and living a life aligned with your values, passions, and unique abilities. It involves self-reflection, introspection, and identifying what truly brings you joy and fulfillment. When you align your actions and choices with your purpose, you can experience a greater sense of meaning and satisfaction in life. Overall, embracing changes, healing from trauma, and elevating into your purpose are interconnected and contribute to personal growth, resilience, and living a more fulfilling life.

Journal Reflection: *Forgiveness is for You*

June 30, 2023

FREEDOM!

This morning, I dropped Gino to school to find his teacher's handicapped child in the wheelchair. Gino took it upon himself to push the child around the classroom, pause, and attempt to make happy faces to get a reaction out of the child. Gino expresses so much love and compassion through his actions. As his current verbal limitations do not interfere with the unconditional love he is. His actions instantly gave me an EPIPHANY; it was the confirmation that not only was my son a PURE angel but most importantly Gino is the representation of my HEART in physical form. How so? In my spiritual lenses, I identified the opportunity to FORGIVE—Kamal Elsayed (father of my sons) To completely see how the handicapped child was in her divine path with physical limitations as my limited verbal son moved with the intentions of love.

Although my son did not say " I care for you" he clearly showed it through his actions. Even when the child did not express gratitude through reciprocation of movement or facial expression, it did not mean that she did not feel the attention and care my son gave her. I met Kamal on the path in which he was handicapped and needed assistance, support, and unconditional love to elevate to his purpose. I gained the clarity that God ordained my assignment in his life to awaken and elevate him through my actions.

This epiphany allowed me to release all the pain, burdens, and hurt that Kamal caused through his limitations. I realized that both Gino and the other child had different levels of restrictions. It only confirmed that we all are the same and handle our battles differently as each lesson will be interpreted and viewed in its unique way by the individual depending on the mindset and frequency that it occurs in one's lifetime. In the past I have forgiven Kamal many times—but TODAY I have completely forgiven him because I truly forgave myself. I forgive myself for accepting the bare minimum my entire life, I forgive myself for not valuing nor seeing my worth, and I forgive myself for accepting my fears, doubts, and worries more than my visions, capabilities, and dreams. I forgive myself for MANY reasons today. This powerful spiritual reflection reached a profound movement within myself in which I felt compelled to text Kamal stating "Safe travels this weekend.

And in case you forgot—I forgive you; may you continue along this journey with a grateful heart, clear mind, and clean spirit. Always encouraging you to do the right things and learn each day from the lessons that you've endured! God bless you!" The emotional release that occurred in that moment is the mental description of being released from jail. I am free! Today I am new! I surrender to the new elevations in all aspects of my life. God said, "My sweet daughter, you passed." There are not enough words to describe this encounter. The real question is—What if Gino's purpose was to save me like he did today? Many things aren't meant to be understood until it's time to be understood. Sometimes it's not meant for us to understand as God blesses us with that understanding. Despite all the hard times I've been physically going through—the ability to see through your spiritual lenses is what makes the difference and allows me to push through each day. This is the gift. I am the prize!

By practicing forgiveness, we create a positive internal environment that aligns with our desires and aspirations. It enables us to let go of negativity, heal, grow, and embrace the opportunities that come our way. It is a conscious choice, a deliberate act of releasing resentment, anger, and the desire for revenge. Ultimately, forgiveness allows us to experience greater joy, peace, and fulfillment as we pave the way for healing and transformation in our lives.

Different Ways to Practice Forgiveness

1 **Self-Reflection and Acceptance:** Start by reflecting on your own emotions and accepting them without judgment. Acknowledge the pain and hurt you feel, and understand that it's normal to experience these emotions.

2 **Empathy and Compassion:** Try to see the situation from the perspective of the person who wronged you. Cultivating empathy and compassion can help you understand their motivations and circumstances, making it easier to forgive.

3 **Writing a Forgiveness Letter:** Consider writing a letter to the person you want to forgive, expressing your feelings and intentions. This exercise can be cathartic and help you articulate your emotions effectively.

4 **Mindfulness and Meditation**: Engage in mindfulness practices and meditation to cultivate awareness of your thoughts and emotions. These practices can help you observe your feelings without getting overwhelmed by them, making it easier to forgive.

5 **Seeking Support**: Don't hesitate to seek support from friends, family, or a therapist. Talking about your feelings and receiving guidance from others can provide you with additional perspectives and insights on forgiveness.

6 **Letting Go of Resentment:** Practice letting go of resentment by consciously choosing not to dwell on past grievances. Focus on the present moment and redirect your energy towards positive thoughts and actions.

7 **Setting Boundaries:** Forgiveness doesn't mean allowing others to continue hurting you. Setting healthy boundaries is essential for self-care and protecting yourself from future harm while still practicing forgiveness.

8 **Engaging in Acts of Kindness:** Channel your forgiveness into acts of kindness and compassion towards others. By spreading positivity and goodwill, you not only benefit those around you but also reinforce your commitment to forgiveness.

Remember, forgiveness is a journey, not a destination. It requires patience, self-reflection, and practice. By embracing forgiveness in all its forms, you open yourself up to a world of healing, growth, and endless possibilities.

Forgiveness indeed has a transformative power that can bring internal freedom and create space for receiving our desires outwardly. Internal Freedom and Forgiveness allow us to release the burden of resentment, anger, or hurt that we may carry within. By forgiving ourselves or others, we let go of negative emotions and free ourselves from the weight of the past. This internal freedom brings peace of mind, emotional well-being, and the ability to move forward with a more positive outlook. Forgiveness is a process of healing. By acknowledging and accepting the pain caused by ourselves or others, we can begin to heal emotional wounds. This healing process enables personal growth, as it encourages self-reflection, empathy, and understanding. Through forgiveness, we can learn lessons, gain wisdom, and evolve as individuals.

When we hold onto grudges or resentment, we often close ourselves off from receiving positive experiences and opportunities. Forgiveness creates space within us, allowing us to be more open and receptive to the good that life has to offer. It opens the door for new relationships, possibilities, and the fulfillment of our desires. Forgiveness plays a vital role in repairing and strengthening relationships. By extending forgiveness to others and ourselves, we foster understanding, empathy, and compassion. This promotes healthier and more authentic connections with others, leading to more fulfilling relationships in our lives.

Gina G Reflections

Whom do you desire to forgive today? What aspects of your past do you seek to let go of today to create room for fresh beginnings?

Chapter 7

The Power of Gratitude

Gratitude can indeed bring a sense of abundance into our lives. When we appreciate the things we have, the people around us, and the experiences we've had, it creates a positive mindset and a greater awareness of the richness in our lives. By focusing on gratitude, we can cultivate a sense of abundance and attract more positivity into our daily experiences. In a world filled with distractions and challenges, the simple act of gratitude can serve as a beacon of light, illuminating the abundance that surrounds us. By embracing gratitude for what we have, whom we cherish, and the moments that shape us, we unlock a profound sense of contentment and awareness. This chapter delves into the transformative power of gratitude, exploring how it can enrich our lives, foster positivity, and pave the way for a more fulfilling existence. We will explore how practicing gratitude can enhance our mental well-being, strengthen relationships, and even boost physical health. By sharing real-life examples, I aim to illustrate how the transformative power of gratitude has shaped my perspectives and overall quality of life; with a deeper understanding of the significance of gratitude and be equipped with tools to harness its potential to create a more fulfilling and enriching life for themselves.

While acknowledging the overwhelming changes in my life—divorce, moving back home with children, the impact of COVID-19, a new job position, and a child's autism diagnosis—I found myself grappling with the weight of these transitions and the emotional turmoil they brought, all while navigating the complexities of daily life and the fears of an uncertain future. Despite feeling lost and uncertain, I trust in God's guidance while pleading for strength for my mind, body, and spirit reflects a desire for resilience in the face of adversity. By asking for divine intervention throughout the shaping of experiences for my healing and growth, I try to embody a profound faith and hope for better days ahead.

Journal Reflection: *One Step at a Time*

March 11, 2019

Dear God,

I don't know what's next in this season, but I trust you. Amid a divorce, moving back home with two kids, the world slowly shutting down due to COVID-19, starting a new position at work, and identifying one child who is autistic and needs support, feels like my life has collapsed. I don't know where to begin, what to do, where to go, how to think, who to see, and when to move forward. I am the ultimate merge in cycles of endings and new beginnings demonstrated in human form. God, I need your help, please strengthen my mind, body, and spirit to proceed with this reality. Please ordain my steps where people, places, and things contribute toward my journey. Allow this experience of mine to heal me and impact those around me.

I trust you.

Separation and Divorce Process Will Stretch You

The difficulties with the separation/divorce process can include emotional turmoil, financial strain, legal complexities, co-parenting challenges, and the overall stress of untangling shared lives. Each situation is unique and can involve a range of complexities that may prolong the process and make it more challenging for all parties involved.

In the tumultuous period of separation and divorce, my primary focus was on fostering an environment of peace and mutual respect. I believed that by prioritizing these values, I could lay a solid foundation for a healthy co-parenting relationship. This meant approaching each interaction with mindfulness, empathy, and a commitment to effective communication. I strived to keep the well-being of our children at the forefront of all decisions and actions, understanding that their emotional stability and security were paramount. Through open dialogue, compromise, and a willingness to put aside personal grievances, I worked towards building a cooperative and harmonious co-parenting dynamic that would benefit not only my children but also both myself and my ex-partner in the long run. This journey was not without its challenges, but by persisting with patience, understanding, and a shared goal of providing a stable and nurturing environment for our children, I found that our efforts to prioritize peace and respect during this difficult time paid off in the form of a stronger, more resilient co-parenting relationship.

Here are a few key highlights that I believe can enhance a healthy co-parenting relationship:

1 **Effective Communication:** Open, honest, and respectful communication is key. Clearly express your thoughts, listen actively, and work together to find solutions.

2 **Co-Parenting Apps:** Utilize co-parenting apps like Our Family Wizard or Coparently to manage schedules, share important information, and communicate effectively.

3 **Consistent Routine:** Establishing a consistent routine for the children can help provide stability and predictability in their lives.

4 **Respect Boundaries:** Respect each other's boundaries and parenting styles. Avoid interfering with each other's time with the children or criticizing each other's decisions.

5 **Flexibility:** Be willing to be flexible and accommodating when unexpected situations arise, such as changes in schedules or emergencies.

6 **Therapy or Mediation:** Consider seeking the help of a therapist or mediator to facilitate discussions and resolve conflicts neutrally and constructively.

7 **Focus on the Children:** Keep the children's best interests at the forefront of all decisions and actions. Work together to create a positive and nurturing environment for them.

8 **Self-care:** Take care of yourself physically, mentally, and emotionally. A healthy co-parent is better equipped to handle the challenges of co-parenting effectively.

9 **Positive Reinforcement:** Acknowledge and appreciate each other's efforts in co-parenting. Celebrate successes and milestones together.

10 **Legal Agreements:** If necessary, establish clear and detailed legal agreements regarding custody, visitation, and other co-parenting arrangements to prevent misunderstandings and conflicts.

My Autistic Child Helps Me See Rainbows and Shooting Stars

Being a parent of an autistic child can present various challenges. These might include difficulties with communication, social interactions, sensory sensitivities, and behavior management. The process involves understanding and accepting the diagnosis, advocating for your child's needs, seeking appropriate therapies and interventions, building a support network, and adapting parenting strategies to meet your child's unique needs. Parents need to educate themselves about autism, practice patience, and prioritize self-care to effectively support their child's development and well-being while fostering a loving and accepting environment at home are also crucial aspects of the parenting journey with an autistic child.

Journal Reflection: *Acceptance to Achievements*

February 14, 2021

To my Dearest Autistic Child,

As I observed you sitting there, isolated and alone, my heart couldn't bear the thought of you feeling lonely, so I stepped in to be your companion. Witnessing that fear in your eyes, devoid of a smile, prompted me to offer you mine, as a beacon of comfort and solace. When the task of tying your shoes seemed insurmountable, I knelt beside you, extending a helping hand to make things a little easier.

Your selective eating habits did not go unnoticed, and I took it upon myself to prepare meals that brought you joy and comfort. Your anxiety about the uncertainties of life weighed heavily on you, so I made it my mission to instill in you a sense of confidence and assurance. When sleep eluded you in the darkness of the night, we found solace in counting the stars together, creating moments of peace and tranquility.

Your unease in the presence of others did not go unheeded, and I stood beside you as your unwavering ally, offering support and understanding. Your struggles to articulate those three simple words, "I love you," did not fall on deaf ears, for I speak to them not just for myself, but for both of us, bridging any gaps left by unspoken words.

The challenges that life has presented you with may seem insurmountable at times, but know this—I am here, steadfast and unwavering, ready to face each hurdle by your side, always and forevermore.

With all my love and unwavering support,

Your Mother.

I understand that many of you may be parenting a child on the autism spectrum, and I want to share some valuable tools and resources that can offer support and guidance. Navigating this journey can be challenging, but these resources can help make the experience a bit easier and more manageable. Here's a list of some helpful options:

1. **Parent Training Programs:** Programs like the Positive Parenting Program (Triple P) offer strategies and support for parents of children with autism.

2. **Support Groups:** Joining support groups for parents of children with autism can provide a sense of community, shared experiences, and valuable advice.

3. **Online Resources:** Websites like Autism Speaks, Autism Society and The National Autistic Society

offer information, resources, and support for parents.

4 **Therapy Services:** Accessing therapy services such as behavioral therapy, speech therapy, and occupational therapy can help children with autism reach their full potential.

5 **Educational Advocacy:** Understanding your child's educational rights and advocating for appropriate services and accommodations in school settings can be crucial.

6 **Respite Care:** Seeking respite care services can provide parents with a much-needed break and support in caring for their child.

7 **Applied Behavior Analysis (ABA):** ABA therapy is an evidence-based intervention that can help children with autism improve social, communication, and behavioral skills.

8 **Parent Coaching:** Working with a parent coach or counselor who specializes in autism can provide personalized support and strategies for managing challenges.

9 **Sibling Support:** Programs that offer support and resources for siblings of children with autism can help promote understanding and positive sibling relationships.

10 **Self-Care:** Taking care of your own physical, mental, and emotional well-being is crucial. Make

time for self-care activities and seek support when needed.

Experience with New Position and Work Balance

The decision to leave a career job in favor of a position that aligns with one's children's schedule is a significant life choice that can come with a multitude of challenges and rewards. This transition often requires individuals to prioritize their family's needs over their career aspirations, leading to a temporary sacrifice of personal passions for the greater good. As one delves into the world of balancing motherhood with professional responsibilities, a complex web of emotions and experiences unfolds.

The sacrifices made along the journey of motherhood can sometimes lead to feelings of isolation and a lack of belonging as one navigates through uncharted territories. Rapid changes in both home and work environments can further complicate this delicate balance, making it challenging to meet the high demands of parental responsibilities and a new work setting simultaneously. The struggle to find a balance between personal well-being and the needs of others can be overwhelming, particularly when compounded by the physical and mental strain of sleep deprivation.

Yet, within this turmoil, a glimmer of hope emerges through the power of positivity. By embracing a resilient mindset and a can-do attitude, I was able to adapt to new circumstances, push through the difficulties, and navigate the uncharted waters ahead. This journey of adaptation and growth opens doors to new opportunities and challenges that not only shape one's role as a parent and a professional but also contribute to personal development and self-discovery. Through perseverance and a willingness to embrace change, I found strength in vulnerability and resilience in the face of adversity, ultimately emerging stronger and more capable of tackling whatever life throws my way.

I know how overwhelming it can be to juggle the demands of work and personal life, especially when you're trying to find balance for yourself and your family. It's essential to create a healthy separation between the two to ensure you're not sacrificing your time or well-being. Here are some practical strategies to help you maintain that balance and prioritize your own needs while managing your responsibilities:

1. **Set Boundaries:** Establish clear boundaries between work and personal life to prevent work from encroaching on your time.

2. **Prioritize Tasks:** Identify and focus on essential tasks first to ensure that you are addressing the most critical responsibilities in both areas.

3. **Schedule Personal Time:** Allocate specific time slots for personal activities and hobbies to ensure you have time for relaxation and enjoyment.

4. **Delegate:** Delegate tasks at work and home whenever possible to lighten your load and free up time for yourself.

5. **Practice Self-Care**: Prioritize self-care activities like exercise, meditation, hobbies, or spending

time with loved ones to maintain your well-being and reduce stress.

I believe setbacks can often serve as wake-up calls, prompting us to reevaluate our priorities and focus on personal growth. These moments can provide opportunities for introspection and self-improvement, ultimately leading to a better understanding of oneself and one's goals. Practicing gratitude has numerous benefits, including improved mental well-being, enhanced self-esteem, better sleep, reduced stress, and stronger relationships. It can also lead to a more optimistic outlook on life and an increased ability to handle challenges.

There are several ways to practice gratitude, such as keeping a gratitude journal, expressing thanks to others, meditating on things you're grateful for, or simply taking time to reflect on the positive aspects of your life. These practices can help cultivate a more appreciative mindset.

1　**Gratitude Journaling:** Writing down things you are grateful for daily can shift your focus towards positivity and abundance.

2　**Expressing Thanks:** Verbally or in writing, expressing gratitude to others fosters appreciation and strengthens relationships, creating a sense of abundance in your social connections.

3　**Mindful Appreciation:** Taking moments throughout the day to appreciate the small things can cultivate a greater awareness of the richness in your life.

4 **Gratitude Meditation:** Practicing gratitude meditation can help you center your thoughts on the positive aspects of your life, promoting a sense of abundance and well-being.

5 **Acts of Kindness:** Engaging in acts of kindness towards others can spark gratitude within yourself and create a cycle of abundance through goodwill.

6 **Reflecting on Past Experiences:** Looking back on past challenges and seeing how you've grown can instill a sense of gratitude for your journey and the strength you've gained.

7 **Gratitude Walks:** Taking walks while consciously appreciating the nature and environment around you can enhance your sense of abundance and connection to the world.

8 **Gratitude Rituals:** Incorporating gratitude rituals into your daily routine, such as a morning gratitude practice or an evening reflection, can help reinforce a mindset of abundance.

9 **Gratitude Letters:** Writing letters of appreciation to people who have positively impacted your life can deepen your sense of gratitude and abundance.

10 **Counting Blessings:** Reflecting on the blessings you have, whether material possessions, relationships, or opportunities, can remind you of the abundance in your life and foster a grateful mindset.

By recognizing and valuing what you presently have can create an environment that attracts increase and abundance. When we appreciate and cherish the things, relationships, and opportunities that are already in our lives, we cultivate a positive mindset and energy. This mindset opens us up to receiving more blessings and abundance.

By focusing on gratitude and acknowledging the value of what we have, we create fertile ground for growth and attract more positive experiences into our lives. Gratitude can significantly impact one's mindset and approach to opportunities. Acknowledging and appreciating what one has often opens a mindset that is more receptive to new opportunities and experiences. This mindset can also contribute to a positive outlook, which in turn can attract more success and abundance.

Gina G Reflections

How can you adopt a mindset of gratitude throughout the difficulties and tests that life presents?

Chapter 8

The End is Where You Start

In this chapter, we delve into the profound concept of how endings mark the initiation of new beginnings. By exploring the complexities of surrendering and acknowledging our lack of control over certain aspects of life, we discover a transformative journey of growth and renewal. Through introspection and acceptance, we learn to release our grip on the past and embrace the unknown future with resilience. This chapter serves as a guiding light, illuminating the path toward understanding that every conclusion paves the way for a fresh start. By accepting the nature of endings and beginnings, we are urged to not only accept change but also to actively embrace it as a fundamental element of our ongoing journey of self-discovery and personal development. This profound understanding empowers us to navigate transitions with grace and openness, fostering a mindset that views change as a catalyst for growth and transformation within our unique narratives.

What They Do Has Nothing to Do with You

Finding wisdom in endings involves realizing that other people's mindsets, behaviors, and actions are separate from how you choose to interpret and integrate those experiences into your path of acceptance and growth. In the journey of self-discovery and personal growth, it is crucial to understand that the behaviors and mindsets of others do not define your trajectory along the journey. For instance, if someone close to you reacts negatively to a decision you've made, it's important to recognize that their response reflects their own beliefs and values, not necessarily a judgment of your choices. By acknowledging this distinction, you can maintain clarity and confidence in your path, allowing room for self-acceptance and growth.

Consider a scenario where you receive criticism from a colleague at work for a project you worked on diligently. Instead of internalizing their feedback as a reflection of your capabilities, you can separate their viewpoint from your self-worth. By doing so, you can identify areas for improvement without allowing external opinions to undermine your confidence. Furthermore, in personal relationships, understanding that others' actions are a product of their own experiences can foster empathy and prevent unnecessary conflict. For example, if a friend constantly cancels plans at the last minute, recognizing that their behavior may stem from personal struggles can help you respond with compassion rather than resentment. This mindset shift can lead to healthier interactions and deeper connections. Ultimately, by embracing the idea that external factors do not dictate your internal growth, you can navigate endings with resilience and openness. This mindset empowers you to extract valuable lessons from experiences, cultivate self-awareness, and forge a path of acceptance and elevation that is uniquely your own.

Journal Entry: *Embracing the Wisdom Within*

January 11, 2023

In the depths of our existence lies a profound truth which is the essence of our being resonating with the universe, guiding us through the flows of life. It is in the silence of our souls that we unearth the answers we relentlessly seek, a beacon of light amidst the chaotic journey we endure. The whispers of our soul, gentle and yet resolute, summon us to embrace change, shed the mantle of familiarity, and step into the unknown. It is a call to let go of the past, to release the grip of outdated patterns, and to unfold the wings of transformation.

As we pay attention to the whispers within, we find ourselves at a crossroads, where the decision to move forward is intertwined with the willingness to relinquish the comfort of the known. It is a time of introspection, of peeling away the layers that no longer serve us, of bidding farewell to relationships that have run their course, and of embracing the dawn of new beginnings. In the stillness of our souls, we discover the courage to confront our fears, the strength to confront our vulnerabilities, and the resilience to forge ahead despite the uncertainties that lie ahead.

It is a journey of self-discovery, a pilgrimage of the spirit, where the echoes of our deepest desires echo through the chambers of our hearts. It is a wisdom that transcends the boundaries of logic, a knowing that defies rationality, and a guidance that surpasses the limitations of the material world. So, dear traveler of the soul, listen closely to the whispers that echo within you. For in their soft cadence lies the roadmap to your destiny, the compass to your true north, and the key to unlocking the boundless potential that resides within you. Embrace the silence of your being, for within it lies the infinite wisdom of your soul.

Navigating endings and transitions is an inevitable part of our journey. As we stand at the threshold of change, uncertain and yet resolute, it is essential to arm ourselves with tools that can illuminate the path ahead and nurture our spirits through the winds of transformation.

Journaling, a sacred act of pouring our thoughts onto paper, becomes a sanctuary for our innermost reflections and emotions. It allows us to unravel the tangled threads of our minds, to make sense of the chaos within, and to trace the patterns of our evolving selves. Through the written word, we find solace, clarity, and a sense of release that paves the way for healing and growth.

Mindfulness practices, such as meditation and yoga, serve as anchors in the stormy seas of change. They ground us in the present moment, allowing us to cultivate awareness, acceptance, and resilience in the face of uncertainty. By embracing mindfulness, we learn to ride the waves of transition with grace and poise, finding peace amidst the turbulence of transformation.

Seeking support from friends, loved ones, or a therapist becomes a lifeline in times of transition. Their ears to listen, shoulders to lean on, and words of encouragement provide us with the strength and reassurance we need to weather the storms of change. Through their unwavering presence, we find comfort, understanding, and a sense of belonging that sustains us through the darkest of times.

Setting new goals, no matter how small or grand, becomes a beacon of hope during endings. By envisioning a future filled with possibilities and aspirations, we ignite the spark of motivation within us, propelling us forward toward new horizons and opportunities. With each goal set and achieved, we reaffirm our capacity for growth, resilience, and transformation.

Engaging in self-care activities becomes a balm for our weary souls as we navigate the terrain of change. Whether it be indulging in a soothing bath, taking a leisurely walk in nature, or practicing a hobby that brings us joy, self-care nurtures our spirits and replenishes our energy reserves. Through self-care, we honor our needs, nourish our souls, and cultivate a sense of well-being that sustains us through the ebbs and flows of transition.

Focusing on personal growth becomes the cornerstone of our journey through endings and transitions. It is a commitment to evolving, learning, and expanding our horizons in the face of change. By embracing personal growth, we transform endings into new beginnings, challenges into opportunities, and uncertainties into possibilities. Through personal growth, we emerge stronger, wiser, and more resilient than ever before, ready to embrace the infinite potential that lies within us.

In conclusion, as we stand on the threshold of change, armed with these tools of resilience, wisdom, and self-care, we embark on a journey of transformation that leads us to the depths of our souls and the heights of our aspirations. With each step we take, each breath we breathe, and each moment we embrace, we move closer to the essence of our being, where the whispers of our soul guide us toward our true destiny. Embrace the silence of your being, for within it lies the infinite wisdom of your soul, beckoning you toward a future filled with promise, purpose, and endless possibilities.

Gina G Reflections

In the silence of your being, what has your spirit been whispering to you that you've been ignoring? What steps can you take today to listen wholeheartedly as your new beginnings are manifesting?

Chapter 9

Dream BIG

In this chapter, we delve into the essence of taking some 'L's in life—live, love, learn, laugh, and lean into life—embracing each moment with a spirit of growth and resilience. The L's are dedicated to embracing life's experiences. We embark on a journey of self-discovery and personal growth by exploring interconnected themes: living authentically, loving wholeheartedly, continuously learning, finding joy in laughter, and facing life's challenges with courage and optimism. By reflecting on these principles and integrating them into our daily lives, we aim to cultivate a mindset that fosters resilience, gratitude, and a deeper connection to the world around us. Through the lens of these fundamental values, we seek to navigate the complexities of existence with grace, purpose, and a newfound appreciation for the beauty of the human experience.

Embrace the idea that you are exactly where you need to be in this moment. Allow yourself to enjoy the anticipation of what lies ahead, trusting that everything will happen at the right time. The upcoming "L's" will affirm your intuition, offering clear signs that you are on the right path. As we embrace the concept of "Right on Time," we will naturally express peace, presence, trust, joy, and ease. By being grateful for past challenges, we can better appreciate our current blessings and future opportunities. Stay present and maintain your excitement, for there is magic in the now and even greater wonders on the horizon, ready to be shaped by your steadfast presence.

As you continue this journey, trust that more days filled with alignment and fulfillment are on the horizon. You are intricately connected to the unfolding of your destiny, unlocking the secrets of your existence with simplicity and gratitude. Embrace your heart, your truth, and your transformative power, as you step into the life you've always envisioned

For instance, picture a moment when you followed your gut feeling about a job opportunity that led to a fulfilling career path. You trusted the timing and found yourself exactly where you needed to be, experiencing a deep sense of peace and joy. Your presence in that moment was a testament to your inner knowing and alignment with the universe's plan. Consider a time when you faced a challenging situation that tested your resolve. Despite the struggles, you maintained a sense of peace and trust that everything would work out in the end. Through these trials, you learned valuable lessons that shaped your perspective and strengthened your resilience.

Recognize that regardless of the current circumstances or future uncertainties, peace, and joy remain your default setting. Trust in the process, relish the present and yearn for wisdom from every experience, whether high or low. Each moment is a teacher guiding you toward your desires and aspirations. Think back to a time when a setback led you to a breakthrough, opening doors to new possibilities and opportunities you never imagined. Your ability to navigate challenges with grace and gratitude set the stage for the abundance that followed, reinforcing the idea that every experience, whether positive or negative, serves a purpose in your journey of self-discovery and growth.

This is a powerful and inspiring journal reflection on the nature of dreams and the journey toward achieving them. Your message emphasizes the importance of hard work, perseverance, and faith, which are essential elements in turning dreams into reality.

This version maintains the motivational essence while ensuring clarity and fluidity in expression. It encourages action and self-belief, emphasizing the importance of faith and resilience.

Journal Entry: *Dreams Are Real*

November 7, 2017

Only if you dare to dream big enough to turn them into reality. It takes hard work, sacrifice, and consistency to realize and live the life of your dreams. Every dream begins with a thought—a thought that evolves into a vision. The clarity with which you see that vision will determine how closely your dream aligns with reality. Dreams carry messages, perspectives, and energy that guide your everyday decisions, shaping your present. The present, this very moment, is the "now." Remember, the saying that nothing lasts forever is an illusion; you can create experiences in the present that transform into memories lasting a lifetime.

Make every moment count. It's "now or never." Keep in mind that before you took your first breath, your destiny was crafted by the most powerful one—God. Don't give up; surrender and pray. Prayers move mountains, faith flows fountains, and hope brings courage. So, I dare you—I dare you to believe in yourself and step out of your comfort zone. Go out and seize your dreams; don't just stay home and daydream. What are your dreams? Shhh! Don't just talk about them—show yourself that you are capable. Prove to others that you are faithful but be wise about the negativity the world may throw your way to distract you. Stay prayed up and remain covered; that is more essential than a pretty facade. Remember, not everything that glitters is gold. Stay humble, strive with motivation, work hard, and believe—because dreams do come true.

In a world where doubt often overshadows the realm of dreams, this insightful piece beautifully delves into the profound truth that dreams can indeed materialize, guiding us toward our authentic purpose and spiritual essence. Through profound wisdom, the transformative influence of trusting in the invisible encourages us to embrace the enchanting possibilities inherent in our dreams. This work serves as a powerful reminder that our deepest aspirations are not mere illusions but potential realities waiting to be brought to fruition, directing us toward a higher purpose and a deeper comprehension of our being. The ability to dream big kindles the inner flame, serving as a testament to the extraordinary voyage toward self-discovery and the realization of our soul's mission.

In conclusion, all seeds planted, eventually reap, which highlights the profound truth that every effort we sow in life, no matter how small or insignificant it may seem at the time, has the potential to bear fruit in the future. Just like seeds planted in a garden, our actions, intentions, and endeavors have the power to grow and flourish over time, bringing about the harvest of our dreams and aspirations. May the visions and dreams inspire us to plant our seeds of hope, love, and perseverance with unwavering faith, knowing that in the fertile soil of our intentions, a bountiful harvest awaits. Let us cultivate our dreams with care, watered by determination and nourished by resilience, confident that in the fullness of time, we will reap the rewards of our labor and witness the beauty of our efforts come to fruition.

The ability to dream big serves as a reminder to nurture ourselves.

Gina G Reflections

What seeds are you planting in your life today? How are you nurturing them to ensure a bountiful harvest in the future?

Chapter 10

Unconditional Love

Definitions of Love can be varied by the perceptions, experiences, and connections that others have encountered. Love, often considered the purest and most profound of emotions, has been the subject of countless discussions, poems, and songs throughout history. It is a force that transcends boundaries, unites souls, and brings about immense joy and fulfillment. But what is love truly? Love is a complex and multifaceted emotion that has been defined in many ways across cultures and throughout history. Historically, love has also been viewed through the lens of various philosophical and religious perspectives. In Christianity, for instance, love is seen as a divine attribute, emphasizing the importance of agape love—selfless love that seeks the well-being of others. For example, the ancient Greeks identified several types of love, such as:

1. **Eros:** Romantic, passionate love.

2. **Philia:** Affectionate love, often found in friendships.

3. **Storge:** Familial love, the bond between parents and children.

4 **Agape:** Unconditional love, often associated with selflessness and compassion.

In the realm of psychology, love has been studied and associated with the attachment theory, which explores the emotional bonds formed between individuals. This theory highlights the importance of love in human development and relationships.

My Perspective on Love

I believe it is a deep-rooted emotion, a chemical reaction in the brain, or something far more profound and spiritual. In this chapter, we will delve into the concept of unconditional love and explore its transformative power in our lives. Love can be identified as the universal language that has captivated the hearts and minds of humanity for centuries, representing light in the often-tumultuous journey of life. It is perceived as the purest and most profound of emotions, igniting the depths of our souls and inspiring countless works of art, literature, and music.

Love transcends boundaries of culture, time, and space, weaving together the threads of human connection and binding individuals in a diversity of shared experiences. While love is commonly perceived as an emotion, a fluttering of the heart, or a rush of warmth, its essence extends far beyond mere feelings. Is love simply a chemical reaction in the brain, a biological response to stimuli, or does it possess a deeper, more spiritual significance? This chapter embarks on a journey to unravel the enigma of love, particularly focusing on the exploration of unconditional love and its profound impact on our lives.

To me, love is an intricate combination of our perceptions, experiences, and connections. It is not confined to a single definition; rather, it embodies a spectrum of feelings and actions that nurture and uplift us. Love can manifest as the warmth of a friend's support, the bond between family members, or the passionate connection shared between partners. At its core, love is about understanding and acceptance. It is a willingness to see others for who they are, to embrace their imperfections, and to stand by them in times of joy and sorrow. Love inspires us to be better versions of ourselves; it propels us to act with kindness, empathy, and compassion.

I believe that love is transformative. It has the power to heal wounds and bridge divides, fostering connections in a world that often feels fragmented. In moments of love, we find a sense of belonging and purpose, as our hearts open to the beauty of human connection. Love is both a feeling and an action. It is expressed through our words, our choices, and the time we dedicate to those we hold dear. It is a journey, not a destination—a continuous exploration of what it means to connect deeply with ourselves and others. In a world that can sometimes feel chaotic, love remains a guiding light, reminding us of our shared humanity and the profound joy that comes from genuine connection.

Representation of Love is to Seek God from Within

Unconditional love often appears as a love that flows freely, unselfconsciously by personal gain or self-interest. This rare and transformative form of love challenges us to look beyond the superficial and embrace the essence of another being, flaws and all. It beckons us to see the divinity within everyone, recognizing that we are all interconnected in a vast web of existence. As we navigate the intricate landscape of love, we are compelled to ponder its significance in our lives. How does unconditional love shape our relationships, our interactions, and our understanding of the world around us? Through introspection and exploration, we begin to uncover the profound truth that love is not merely an emotion or a fleeting sensation; it is a guiding force, a source of strength and resilience that empowers us to transcend our limitations and embrace the fullness of our humanity.

Unconditional love, at its core, is a love that knows no bounds, no conditions, and no expectations. It is a love that is pure, selfless, and all-encompassing. In seeking to understand unconditional love, we are often led to the idea of seeking God within ourselves. Many spiritual traditions and teachings emphasize the connection between love and divinity, suggesting that to truly love others unconditionally, we must first find that divine spark of love within ourselves. By recognizing the presence of God or the divine within us, we are better able to extend that same unconditional love to others, fostering deeper connections and understanding in our relationships.

Journal Entry: *Lead with Love Poem*

February 14, 2023

In every moment, let love be your guide,
A beacon of light, shining far and wide.
With each action and every word you say,
Let love lead the path in every single way.
Imagine the power when love takes the lead,
Transforming each thought, each word, each deed.
Your presence is a beacon in the darkest night,
Spreading warmth and compassion, shining bright.
Choosing love isn't just for you alone,
It sets a stage where seeds of kindness are sown.
A ripple of positivity, spreading wide and far,
Healing wounds, lighting up where shadows are.
Love as your compass, your guiding star,
Opening doors to a life that knows no bar.
Embracing joy, nurturing peace every day,
Let love lead the way, come what may.

Poem Insights

Leading with love empowers your choices by transforming everyday moments into opportunities for positive impact. When love guides your decisions, you are more likely to prioritize compassion and kindness, making a difference in the lives of others and yourself.

Love strengthens connections by building bridges and fostering understanding in relationships and communities.

It creates a sense of unity and empathy that transcends differences, leading to stronger bonds and a more harmonious environment for everyone involved. When you choose to lead with love, you inspire those around you to do the same. Your actions serve as a model for others, creating a ripple effect of positivity that can spread far and wide. By setting an example of love and compassion, you contribute to a more caring and supportive world. Embracing love in your actions enhances your well-being by contributing to emotional health. When you act with love, you reduce stress, increase happiness, and cultivate a sense of fulfillment that comes from making a positive impact on the lives of others. This emotional well-being is essential for overall health and happiness, making love a powerful force for personal growth and fulfillment.

In conclusion, Love is the key. Many lost their key trying to find love on this journey. Love is indeed the root of all great things. It is the driving force behind acts of kindness, compassion, and selflessness. When we operate from a place of love, we can transcend our limitations and connect with others on a deeper level. Love is not just an emotion; it is a guiding principle that can lead us towards greater fulfillment and purpose in life. It is said that many have lost their key while trying to find love on this journey, but perhaps the key was within them all along—the key to unconditional love.

Gina G Reflections

As you reflect on the concept of unconditional love, consider the following questions: How can I cultivate more love and compassion in my own life? How can I show up in the form of love while helping others cultivate love in their own lives?

www.ingramcontent.com/pod-product-compliance
Lightning Source LLC
Chambersburg PA
CBHW040811120726
48005CB00012B/1383